# I Feel...
# AWESOME

Words and pictures by

## DJ Corchin

Did you know that
I'm **awesome?**

'Cause I worked out a ton.

I ate all my vegetables.

Even *this* one.

I put away all my toys
after the fun.

But both you and I know
the fun's never done.

I **helped** out a friend
who needed a hand.

I **practiced** my music.

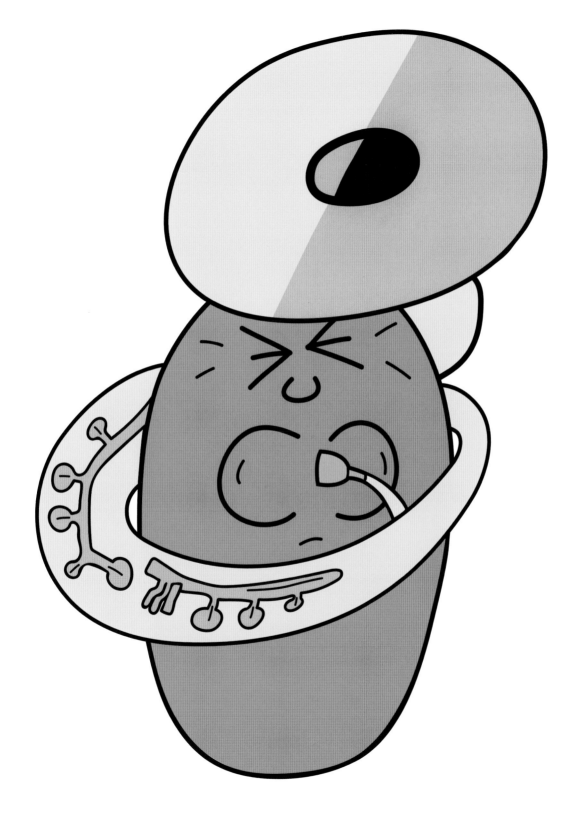

For our rock 'n' roll band.

I **helped** with the cooking
'cause it tasted so bland,

and now my lasagna
is in high demand.

I **included** Miss Susie,
who sat all alone,

not because she was bad,

but because she's all grown.

And none of the kids
seemed to have known

that her stories are **awesome.**
Now their minds are all blown!

# I read all the time.

# I take all my baths.

including my math.

I often say **"thank you"**

and **share** what I have.

If you're **feeling blue,**

I'll **help** you to laugh.

I **love** who I am
and what I can bring.

I just want to **fly**
if you know what I mean.

I feel **super awesome**
'cause I'm doing great things.

# I Feel...
# AWESOME

Who doesn't love to feel AWESOME! It's a totally amazing feeling to have and the best part is there are always things you can do to feel awesome. As in this book, some of those things are about having fun, some are about accomplishing what you need to do, and some of them are about helping others. That feels the best of all!

## Let's explore awesome stuff to do!

## Make an Awesome Box:

1. Grab an extra box. Could be a shoe box, a leftover shipping box, or something else you have in the house. (It works best with something that has a lid.)

2. Decorate the box with your favorite colors using paint, markers, crayons, or all of them at once. Glue pictures of awesome things and people on it. Be sure to label it with "AWESOME BOX." Be as creative as you can!

3. If the box doesn't have a lid, cut a hole in the top so you can get things in and out easily.

4. Once you have your Awesome Box, start filling it with things that make you feel awesome, such as a picture of someone, a rock from a place you love to visit, a note from a friend, a list of ideas to help others, or anything else you can think of!

5. When you have a moment that you're not feeling so awesome, grab your awesome box and dive in.

6. You can keep adding or trading out your awesome items!

# It is ALWAYS OK to ask someone for help when you are feeling bad.

The I Feel... Children's Series is a resource created to assist in discussions about emotional awareness.

Please seek the help of a trained mental healthcare professional and start a discussion today.

## Learn about the past:

1. Pick someone over the age of sixty that is a family member, teacher, or friend you know.

2. Ask them to tell you a story about when they were young that they think of fondly.

3. Using a piece of paper, draw an *I Feel...* oval face of them in their story.

4. Find a friend that is your age and tell them the story you learned and show them your drawing.

5. Ask your friend to find someone over the age of sixty and share their story with you!

## Helping others makes you feel awesome!

1. Get together with three or more friends or family members.

2. Decide if there's a place in your community where people may not be feeling so awesome and discuss the reasons why.

3. Find a charity or organization you can volunteer at that helps those people.

4. Take a trip and spend some time helping those in need.

5. Write down on a piece of paper what you did, who you helped, and how you feel afterwards.

6. Put it in your Awesome Box.

## Getting it done makes you feel awesome!

1. Clean your room cleaner than you've ever cleaned before.

2. Take your bath or shower. It feels so refreshing!

3. Do all your homework.

4. Brush your teeth for two whole minutes.

5. Practice something that you're supposed to practice.

6. What else can you do that needs doing?

## Go to space...AWESOME SPACE!

1. Find an area somewhere in your home or classroom.

2. Decorate it with stars, comets, planets, awesome aliens, and rockets.

3. Add awesome colors, pictures, and art you made.

4. Be sure to have a big wacky sign that says, "AWESOME SPACE."

5. In that area, have fun activities, cool toys, and maybe even your AWESOME BOX.

6. When you're feeling blue or as a reward, take off to AWESOME SPACE!

# To Erin

Published by Sourcebooks eXplore, an imprint of Sourcebooks Kids
P.O. Box 4410, Naperville, Illinois 60567–4410
(630) 961-3900
sourcebookskids.com

Originally published in 2013 in the United States of America by The phazelFOZ Company, LLC.

Library of Congress Cataloging-in-Publication Data is on file with the publisher.

Source of Production: 1010 Printing Asia Limited, North Point, Hong Kong, China
Date of Production: July 2020
Run Number: 5019239

Printed and bound in China.
OGP 10 9 8 7 6 5 4 3 2 1